CO-DEPENDENTS ANONYMOUS

Common Threads of Codependency:

Codependents Talk about Codependency,
Recovery, Relapse, and Authenticity

For general information about CoDA,
please write or call:
Co-Dependents Anonymous, Inc.
P.O. Box 33577
Phoenix, AZ 85067-3577
USA
Phone: 602-277-7991
Toll Free: 888-444-2359
Spanish Toll Free: 888-444-2379
www.coda.org

For additional copies of this booklet, contact:
CoRe Publications
P.O. Box 1004
Denver, NC 28037-1004
USA
Phone: 704-483-3038
Fax: 704-483-3088
E-mail: coreorders@coda.org
Online ordering: www.coda.org/estore

Table of Contents

THE CODEPENDENCY DILEMMA

As codependents we come in different flavors, from martyr to victim, from rebel to doormat. We may have different backgrounds and different issues, but we come to recognize certain traits in ourselves and in each other. Our purpose in this piece of literature is to examine these traits, these common threads of thought and behavior that are interwoven into this complex tapestry we call codependency.

We choose not to define codependency for two reasons. It is not our intent to decide whether or not anyone else is codependent. Our Third Tradition reminds us that the only requirement for membership in CoDA is a desire for healthy and loving relationships. We don't even have to decide that we are codependent before joining Co-Dependents Anonymous. We do not presume to hold the ultimate answer to the codependency question. We simply share our own experience, strength, and hope. Each reader is free to choose what sounds relevant and to discard what does not.

Also, we find that precisely defining codependency is not as useful to us as simply accepting the reality of it. The cause of our codependency is not as important as the fact that it exists. All we need is honesty, an open mind, and willingness to work the program. In this piece, we share some of the common features of our experience as we seek to understand the nature of our own codependency and recovery.

Where did it come from?

Somewhere along the line, we learned to doubt our perceptions, discount our feelings, and overlook our needs. Telling people what we thought or felt often resulted in our being ignored, laughed at, or punished. We looked to others to tell us what to think, what to feel, how to behave. In this way, other people supplied us with information about who we were and who we should be. They defined us and our view of the world, and we may have accepted that as reality. It became more important to be compliant than to be authentic, and we adopted rigid beliefs about what "should be." We believed that if we could just "get it right," things would be okay. We looked to others for the rules that defined us and for assurance that we were " getting it right." Our self-esteem hinged on gaining others' approval. When we "got it wrong," our sense of security and self-worth evaporated.

We saw ourselves as flawed. For many of us, that led to shame, fear, secrecy, dishonesty, manipulation, control, depression, and isolation. Some of us rebelled against rules and authority and became sullen, defensive, or arrogant. As a result of holding these mistaken beliefs about ourselves, we often passed them along to others. When they did not conform, we may have judged them harshly, cultivating blame and resentment, thus perpetuating the cycle of codependency.

We didn't really get to know other people. Our lives became an elaborate play in which we were acting a part. We interacted with others based on how we perceived their roles related to ours. Without an effective internal sense of security or well-being, we were unable to maintain functional relationships. We could not identify with other people as whole human beings. To us, they were just characters in our life story.

Trying to "get it right" cost us dearly. We did not own ourselves. We did not know or trust our own thoughts and feelings. We were unaware of our own contributions to the events in our lives. Hiding our true selves in order to fit in kept us isolated and unable to ask for help. Constantly denying our true thoughts and feelings was stressful and exhausting. We may have used alcohol, drugs, food, nicotine, activities, sex, or preoccupation with others to escape.

Being in denial, we were left with a sense of emptiness. Our relationships became increasingly disappointing. Ultimately, we found ourselves locked into a compulsive pattern of belief and behavior that could not satisfy us.

Members of CoDA answer the question, "How do I describe codependency?"

- "Thinking I have to be perfect to be OK."

- "Codependency is taking your temperature to see how I feel."

- "Having somebody else tell me how to think, feel, see, or do!"

- "Letting myself get swallowed up by others, not knowing what I want, need, or feel."

- "Before CoDA, other people were the focus of my life, confirming who I was."

- "Being true to you as a way of life leaves me not knowing how to be true to me."

- "Focusing on what's wrong with somebody else, not being able to feel happy until they change, and trying to get them to be different, so I can be happy."

- "On a personal level, codependency is whenever I am not in serenity. When I am not satisfied with my state of being, I'll use any manner of thinking and behaving to escape the discomfort of just being. This can range from the mild to the bizarre, from slight discomfort to self-destructive thinking and behavior."

- "I think codependency can be described as being out of balance; i.e. behaviors like not taking care of yourself, being overly concerned with others and having weak boundaries. I don't think the behaviors people identify with codependency are bad, they are just directed in unhealthy ways, or are extremes of healthy behaviors."

- "Codependency, for me, means attempting to give insight to others, trying to control the outcome of a situation for my comfort, and thinking I know best what will make everyone feel better."

- "It means not standing up for myself in healthy, appropriate ways which show respect for myself and the other person."

II. RECOVERY
That First CODA Meeting

Some of us found it difficult to grasp that there was anything wrong with us. We thought that we were "fine." We worked hard to show how fine we were. We did everything "right." We had the right degree, the right job, the right spouse, the right house; and our kids went to the right schools. How could it have gone so wrong? Some of us had a lot of self-doubts. We had come to believe that there was something inherently wrong with us that we had to hide from others. We worked hard to keep them from finding out who we really were, when we didn't even know ourselves.

Our pasts were filled with secrets we dared not share. Whether we are trying to influence or avoid others, we eventually found that something was missing. For all our efforts, we never seemed to find the sense of emotional security and love we craved. We could not see or value our own needs and wants. Instead, we either became consumed with another person; or else, we avoided others as much as possible. No matter what path brought us to our first CoDA meeting, most of us came with a nagging feeling that something was wrong, even if we weren't exactly sure what it was.

Some of us identified with codependency right away. We read the list of "Patterns of Codependence": denial, low self-esteem, compliance, control, avoidance; and we felt our pain was validated. Some of us read the list with puzzlement. Yes, we could identify with it: but we thought--isn't this behavior, well, "normal?" It was hard to grasp that it might be the source of our distress. How could such ordinary behavior and thinking make us feel so crazy? What usually got us to our first CoDA meeting was an unbearable suffering that we could not seem to escape. Often our distress was brought on by a deteriorating or broken relationship.

CoDA members answer the question,
"Why did I start going to CoDA meetings?"

- "Even though I have recovery in another Fellowship, I still felt there was something wrong."

- "My life was crappy, and I figured it couldn't hurt."

- "I started going to CoDA meetings as part of my desperate attempt to find a 'cure' for my codependency and to relieve the misery of a relationship that did not work out."

- "I started going because I was in a lot of pain, with a ton of ambivalent feelings, over one particular relationship. I was looking for hope, answers, a sense of connection with a recovery group, and some real change in my life."

- "I started going because I had just gotten out of an abusive relationship. I knew that something had to change within me if I were going to stay out of that relationship and not jump into another one just like it. All of my romantic relationships up to that point had been troubled, and each one seemed to be worse than the last. I knew something had to change."

- "I kept getting into sick relationships."

- "I knew there was something wrong; I just didn't have a clue. I didn't know what else to do."

- "My partner tried to slash my throat, and I felt sorry for him."

- "I started going to CoDA meetings because I reached the end of my proverbial rope. Psychotherapy alone was not helping. I wanted to learn why I kept choosing abusive relationships and hurting myself, why I was so unhappy, and just didn't 'get it'. It took a crisis situation to make me look beyond psychotherapy for help."

We discover we are not alone

Codependents are not all stamped out of one mold. One thing that keeps us coming back is our identification with other codependents. As we listen and share in CoDA meetings, we begin to discover that others have similiar feelings and behaviors. We hear our own stories coming from the mouths of strangers. Our sense of isolation finally begins to lift.

Member of CoDA answer the question, "What do I recognize in other codependents that we have in common?"

- "An inability to maintain realistically based friendships"

- "Relying on others to get validation"

- "Reacting impulsively or defensively when I feel attacked or devalued"

- "Having low self-esteem, fearing others' disapproval or rejection, valuing others' beliefs more than our own, being easily influenced, being profoundly out of touch with ourselves, and not knowing what it means to take care of ourselves."

- "Usually I take on a false identity or a façade of niceness in order to be liked. I find myself playing a role so I'll be thought of as a particular kind of person. This can change to suit the situation. Sometimes I dislike another person at first, and later realize that I see something in them that I don't like about myself."

- "When I first came to CoDA, getting better meant getting out of an abusive relationship and not getting into another one. Now I am trying to improve other things about myself, like not gauging my success on the values, opinions, and achievements of others. It is a process of refinement."

- "Newcomers often remind me of how I was when I first started. I, too, had firm beliefs that if someone would just tell me what to do, I would do it and get better, I believed that other people thought something was wrong with me. I found it easy to believe the worst about myself and hard to believe anything positive. I thought I was different. Although I didn't know my own thoughts and feelings, I was sure I knew what others thought and felt. Now I recognize in recovering codependents a feeling of being at ease with ourselves and others, clarity of thought, resilience, genuine compassion, and the desire for self-care."

- "The codependent women in my group have the ability to be open with one another about our shameful pasts, and we support each other in recovery. We have all experienced some type of abuse in our childhood or adolescence that led us into a cycle of painful relationships with others and ourselves. We each have codependent traits that protected us when we were too young to defend ourselves However, these traits no longer work well for us as adults. We each want to learn new behaviors, ways of thinking and responding to our environment in order to enjoy life to the fullest. Our hope is to become fully mature adults who have learned how to become authentic."

The alternative to recovery

Codependency is often subtle. It may not appear that choosing recovery is a life or death decision. We believe otherwise. Without recovery, the patterns of codependency that made us miserable enough to get to a meeting would probably have continued unchanged. At best, we might have stayed miserable, wallowing in self-pity and negativity, moving from relationship to relationship in an attempt to find happiness. Or we might have remained in an abusive, unhealthy marriage "for the sake of the kids," not realizing the lesson we were teaching them--that it's all right for others to mistreat us.

We inadvertently set a poor example for our children, encouraging them, through our example, to become people-pleasers, controllers or manipulators. Attempting to make a good impression on the outside world, we may have neglected the emotional and physical needs of those in our care.

Without recovery, the cycle of shame, fear, and low self-esteem often continues into the next generation unchanged. At worst, we could have self-destructed. Codependency can range from despair and depression to hostility and rage. Untreated, codependents can end up hurting themselves or others.

Members of CoDA answer the question, "Without recovery, where would I be today?"

- "I cannot predict what might have happened in a hypothetical situation. I might have become rich and famous. However, my family exhibited self-destructive behaviors including addictions and suicide."

- "I probably would have started drinking again eventually, or turned to other addictive behaviors to bury my feelings."

- "I think I would have continued to be involved in unhealthy and abusive love relationships. Of course, I can't say for sure."

- "All I know is that I had been in a lot of pain before I came to CoDA. I have not had chaos and turmoil in my life since then."

- "Engaging in self-destruction at the hands of people I felt sorry for."

- "Without recovery, I would probably still be depressed, blaming other people and circumstances for my unhappy lot in life."

- "I was on the verge of suicide before I came to CoDA. I don't know whether or not I would have succeeded in killing myself, but I know that I was desperate. The people around me were miserable and couldn't understand my volatile behavior. I blamed them all for how I felt, although I couldn't honestly communicate with any of them. My life at home and at work was disintegrating. I couldn't keep up the façade any more. Without recovery, I feel certain I would have lost my marriage, my job, and ultimately my life."

Meetings

As codependency led to problems within our relationships, isolating and hiding our true selves no longer worked. We began to realize the benefit of belonging to a group, a place to try out and experience healthy relationships. As we practiced our program and listened to other recovering codependents, we began to understand that, perhaps, our defenses were no longer necessary. We realized that much of our pain and fear was based on beliefs about others and ourselves that simply were not true. Many of us learned that much of what we thought was true about ourselves and our lives was someone else's opinion, one we hadn't thought to question.

Over time, we began to understand how the patterns of codependency were causing us pain. We continued going to CoDA meetings and practicing the program. The more we learned about our own dysfunctional and self-destructive patterns, the more we became able to replace old behaviors with newer, healthier ones.

Many of us experienced the "pink cloud" of early recovery, feeling wonderful from identifying with other codependents. We learned quickly about codependency, no longer feeling alone or defective, having real hope. For many of us, the meeting provided our first experience with sanity; it became our first Higher Power. Then, somewhere along the way, some of us "hit the wall" commonly characterized by the sentiment of not getting anything out of meetings. Those of us who persisted realized we had still been seeking our answers and our definition from other people. We had substituted the meeting group for our parents, friends, lovers, etc. We eventually accepted that the group could not provide us with the security, identity, and answers we sought. Although others in the program could support us on our journey of self-discovery, we also needed to look within ourselves to find our own personal truths. The group was no longer our Higher Power, but rather a community of other recovering people with whom we could be ourselves, without seeking approval and validation. We may have started going to CoDA meetings because we were looking for a one-time cure. We keep going because we find ongoing reinforcement in a program that supports our spiritual and personal growth on our journey towards authenticity.

CoDA Members answer the question, "Why do I continue to go to CoDA meetings?"

- "I haven't been cured; I've been cared for, and my life is better."

- "No matter what's happening in my life, I'm happier since I've been working the Twelve Steps than I ever was before."

- "When I ease up from working the program, I'm depriving myself. I mean if I win the lotto, I'm not going to stop buying tickets! Just because I'm better, I don't have to quit. I can keep on getting better.

- "I have to stay in those places that help me."

- "It's never a bad idea to go to a meeting."

- "Recovery is a learned skill, kind of like learning a foreign language. If I don't practice regularly, I forget some of the words."

- "As I started to get a little recovery and settle down, I was guided by circumstances (Higher Power) into some service work and commitment. Today I am more drawn to meetings by a desire to be of service. In times of stress or relapse, the meetings truly help me see a broader and clearer picture of reality."

- "By going to meetings, I continue learning, connecting, and reminding myself that I have a duty to take care of myself."

- "I go now because I love the fellowship and prayers so much; I also love going because it gives me a chance to reflect, take my inventory, and unload whatever may be burdening my heart."

- "Continued examination of myself and my motivations."

- "Continue my recovery in learning to accept myself."

- "I go for a lot of reasons. Meetings keep me on track. Newcomers remind me of where I was before CoDA, and where I could be again if I drop CoDA. Old timers and readings remind me of the wisdom of the program which I sometimes forget in the rush of daily living."

- "I can be authentic and share in a CoDA meeting as in no other place. One hour without crosstalk may be the most peaceful and restorative experience of my whole week. I experience conscious contact with my Higher Power in meetings."

- "Meetings provide an opportunity for me to carry the message."

- "I have been going to CoDA for five months now. I continue to go because of the growth and healing I experience. Not only have I gained insight into the roots of my behavior, but also I've learned how to behave and think in a healthier manner. The members of my group relate to me, empathize, and most importantly, do not judge me."

- "I can be honest in these meetings. I find true healing and compassion for others and myself, including those who abused me, without caretaking or denying myself. I am learning to let go of the past and embrace the present, knowing that the future will be better because I have changed."

- "CoDA is helping me learn to recognize healthy relationships."

- "I am taking responsibility for myself, finding joy in my life. I no longer feel helpless to escape from the prison of my despair. Recovery, for me, has meant more than attendance at meetings. It involves hard work and the commitment to look deep inside myself and embrace change. A support group like CoDA allows me to know I'm not alone, that others can relate to me because they have been where I have been. I no longer feel crazy or deficient. I am valuable and capable of positive change. For me, attending meetings alone could not do the job. I had to take responsibility for changing myself."

III. RELAPSE
Recognizing a slip or relapse

The CoDA "Welcome" reminds us that codependency is a "deeply rooted, compulsive behavior." We call ourselves "recovering" codependents because recovery is an ongoing process. For every two steps forward, we sometimes take a step back. At times we slip back into old codependent beliefs and behaviors. Often we find ourselves caught by surprise. Suddenly we find ourselves feeling miserable again, and we didn't even recognize what was happening. Although we may perceive that we've slipped, the reality is that we have often chosen behaviors or made decisions that led to relapse. We may not yet have acknowledged these beliefs and behaviors as being codependent. We may engage in old behaviors because we want to believe that this time the outcome will be different. Perhaps it's just easier in the short run. Other times, we simply get blindsided; and we find ourselves swept up again in an old, compulsive pattern over which we feel we have no control. In any case, our program is one of progress, not perfection. Ultimately, a relapse into old, codependent behaviors becomes an opportunity to work toward a new level of recovery.

Combating relapse

To avoid relapse, we need to be aware of what triggers the flood of feelings that erodes our self-esteem. For example, seeing happy couples and families may trigger feelings of jealousy, insecurity, or depression. Or, returning home for holiday gatherings may be threatening, causing us to revert to old behaviors and attitudes. We need to be extra cautious when feeling vulnerable; we may need to avoid certain people and situations that endanger our progress.

Some relapses are brief: and we're able to get back on track with a little help from our group, our sponsor, and trusted friends. Other relapses are more complicated, and we may lose focus as our lives once again become unmanageable (Step One). We need to have a plan to counter the compulsion to behave in old ways. One way is to turn to the Steps, seeing where we need to address our attention. Maybe we can benefit by doing an inventory (Step Ten).

We can ask for knowledge of our Higher Power's will for our lives (Step Eleven). We can talk to our sponsors, attend meetings even when we don't feel like going, and use the meeting's phone list. We can re-read the "Twelve Promises," reminding ourselves that we "can expect a miraculous change in our lives by working the program." Listening to tapes, writing in a journal, practicing deep breathing, and reciting the Serenity Prayer are other methods for combating relapse. We have many recovery tools at our disposal that can help us on the path to recovery and spiritual awakening. Relapse can be serious, but by working our program and using the CoDA tools, we find hope and recovery.

Members of CoDA answer the question, "How do I know I'm in relapse?"

- "I find excuses not to go to meetings."

- "Essentially, when I'm going against my heart."

- "I feel compulsive. Things don't flow anymore."

- "I don't feel good inside. Taking care of myself doesn't feel so great."

- "I'm either living in the past or projecting into the future."

- "I think in black and white."

- "I feel sorry for myself."

- "I feel crazy."

- "There is something wrong with me that no one else can know about."

- "I feel sad for no reason."

- "I worry about little things."

- "My happiness depends on the actions of others."

- "I don't feel content. There is a nagging restlessness. I'm irritable; I'm wrapped up in someone else's problems, and I want to fix everyone's problems."

- "I'm uncomfortable in my own skin."

- "I don't want to feel. I want to escape my feelings."

- "My life becomes unmanageable when I fall back on old behaviors."

IV. AUTHENTICITY
How do we become our authentic selves?

It is not enough for us to hear, "stop practicing codependent behavior," or "stop acting codependently." It seems so vague. We want to know exactly what to do. How do we care without crossing the line into caretaking? How can we be responsible without becoming controlling?

The First Step offers guidance about which behaviors to stop. We admit that we have been attempting by action or thought to have power over others. As long as we are focused on what is wrong with someone else, we cannot work on ourselves.

We have to stop attempting to exert power over other people or wishing another person would change so we could be happy. We also need to be aware of passive attempts to control, such as being a martyr, inducing guilt, manipulating others, or allowing others to mistreat us.

CoDA's "Welcome" also reveals behaviors we need to stop; "We attempted to use others -- our mates, friends, and even our children, as our sole source of identity, value, and well-being, and as a way of trying to restore within us the emotional losses from our childhoods." We have repeatedly sought out relationships to boost our egos, to confirm our identities, and to make us feel good about ourselves. In order to be authentic, we cannot use other people to define who we are and fulfill us. By recognizing our true value, we can stop neglecting and mistreating ourselves. To be true to ourselves, we look inside to find our answers. We turn to our Higher Power. By trusting that we will be taken care of, we begin to heal. At this point, we begin to know a new level of serenity. We discover within ourselves a sense of security and self-worth not bound by anyone else's opinion of us. As we continue to share at meetings, talk with others in the program. and gain insights from our Fourth Step inventory, we become more authentic.

CoDA Members answer the question, "What does being authentic mean to me?"

- "I know who I am today. I genuinely like myself."

- "It means being aware of my feelings as I'm experiencing them and being able to make decisions on whether or not I want to act on them. I don't play Monday morning quarterback with my feelings anymore."

- "As my life in recovery becomes more manageable, I remain in 'conscious contact' with my Higher Power throughout my day. In this way, I am able to slow down long enough to listen to my inner voice of wisdom."

- "I find I'm able to 'carry the message' without giving advice and without expectations, sharing only my experience, strength and hope."

- "Making amends as situations happen, instead of accumulating a 'to do' list for the future."

- "I came to realize that I really can't please everyone, and I cannot expect everyone to like me. As long as my behaviors are consistent with my thoughts and feelings, I am content to be who I am."

- "It means pushing through the fear and saying what's on my mind, being direct instead of being manipulative."

- "When others hurt my feelings, I ask myself, 'What are my intentions?' If they meant to be hurtful, then I ask my Higher

Power to help me 'rise above it.' Maybe they're having a bad day. If what they said was meant to be helpful, I'm able to ask myself, 'Is there something here I need to look at?'"

- "When things go wrong in my life, I stop and ask myself, 'What am I supposed to learn from this experience.' I try to see the positive in each situation, viewing life's ups and downs as an opportunity to grow and practice my new skills."

- "I accept the parts of me that aren't perfect."

- "Having a relationship with my Higher Power."

- "To me, authenticity is serenity and happiness for no reason. I feel content to just be. No one else can affect this feeling. I feel no need to react."

- "Being authentic means being myself as fully and clearly as possible, knowing and expressing my feelings, handling issues with serenity and grace."

- "It's about taking care of my own needs."

- "Trying my best to be healthy and do God's will is a one day at a time journey. I don't think I will ever say. "Okay, now I don't practice any codependent behaviors at all." For me, it is more about working on healthy behaviors."

- "Authenticity isn't about being perfect or not having feelings. It's about balance and sanity in my relationships and my life. It's about using the Steps and Traditions as the guiding principles in all my affairs."

- "It's about minding my own business instead of everyone else's."

V. CONCLUSION

Sometimes it seems that everyone must be codependent, or that codependency is something different for each person. Yet, those of us who have found a more satisfying way of life in the program of Co-Dependents Anonymous have found that we share things in common, both problems and solutions. Our questions are answered as we become more immersed in the program of Co-Dependents Anonymous. We find our answers as we turn to the Steps and Traditions, the experiences of others in CoDA, a relationship with our Higher Power, and our own inner guidance.

PATTERNS AND CHARACTERISTICS
OF CODEPENDENCE

These patterns and characteristics are offered as a tool to aid in self-evaluation. They may be particularly helpful to newcomers.

Denial Patterns:
Codependents often . . .
- have difficulty identifying what they are feeling.
- minimize, alter, or deny how they truly feel.
- perceive themselves as completely unselfish and dedicated to the well-being of others.
- lack empathy for the feelings and needs of others.
- label others with their negative traits.
- think they can take care of themselves without any help from others.
- mask pain in various ways such as anger, humor, or isolation.
- express negativity or aggression in indirect and passive ways.
- do not recognize the unavailability of those people to whom they are attracted.

Low Self-esteem Patterns:
Codependents often . . .
- have difficulty making decisions.
- judge what they think, say, or do harshly, as never good enough.
- are embarrassed to receive recognition, praise, or gifts.
- value others' approval of their thinking, feelings, and behavior over their own.
- do not perceive themselves as lovable or worthwhile persons.
- seek recognition and praise to overcome feeling less than.
- have difficulty admitting a mistake.
- need to appear to be right in the eyes of others and may even lie to look good.
- are unable to identify or ask for what they need and want.
- perceive themselves as superior to others.

- look to others to provide their sense of safety.
- have difficulty getting started, meeting deadlines, and completing projects.
- have trouble setting healthy priorities and boundaries.

Compliance Patterns:
Codependents often . . .
- are extremely loyal, remaining in harmful situations too long.
- compromise their own values and integrity to avoid rejection or anger.
- put aside their own interests in order to do what others want.
- are hypervigilant regarding the feelings of others and take on those feelings.
- are afraid to express their beliefs, opinions, and feelings when they differ from those of others.
- accept sexual attention when they want love.
- make decisions without regard to the consequences.
- give up their truth to gain the approval of others or to avoid change.

Control Patterns:
Codependents often . . .
- believe people are incapable of taking care of themselves.
- attempt to convince others what to think, do, or feel.
- freely offer advice and direction without being asked.
- become resentful when others decline their help or reject their advice.
- lavish gifts and favors on those they want to influence.
- use sexual attention to gain approval and acceptance.
- have to feel needed in order to have a relationship with others.
- demand that their needs be met by others.
- use charm and charisma to convince others of their capacity to be caring and compassionate.
- use blame and shame to exploit others emotionally.
- refuse to cooperate, compromise, or negotiate.

- adopt an attitude of indifference, helplessness, authority, or rage to manipulate outcomes.
- use recovery jargon in an attempt to control the behavior of others.
- pretend to agree with others to get what they want.

Avoidance Patterns:
Codependents often . . .
- act in ways that invite others to reject, shame, or express anger toward them.
- judge harshly what others think, say, or do.
- avoid emotional, physical, or sexual intimacy as a way to maintain distance.
- allow addictions to people, places, and things to distract them from achieving intimacy in relationships.
- use indirect or evasive communication to avoid conflict or confrontation.
- diminish their capacity to have healthy relationships by declining to use the tools of recovery.
- suppress their feelings or needs to avoid feeling vulnerable.
- pull people toward them, but when others get close, push them away.
- refuse to give up their self-will to avoid surrendering to a power greater than themselves.
- believe displays of emotion are a sign of weakness.
- withhold expressions of appreciation.

Notes:

Notes:

Notes:

Notes: